Newly Revised

RECIPES
FOR
ART *and* CRAFT
MATERIALS

Newly Revised

RECIPES
FOR
ART *and* CRAFT
MATERIALS

HELEN RONEY SATTLER

NEW ILLUSTRATIONS BY MARTI SHOHET

LOTHROP, LEE & SHEPARD BOOKS · NEW YORK

Second Edition   4   5   6   7   8   9   10

Library of Congress Cataloging in Publication Data
Sattler, Helen Roney. Recipes for art and craft materials.
Includes index. Summary: Instructions for making pastes, modeling compounds, papier-mâché, paints, inks, and numerous other materials for art and craft work.   1. Handicraft—Equipment and supplies—Juvenile literature.   2. Artists' materials—Formulae, tables, etc.—Juvenile literature.   [1. Handicraft—Equipment and supplies.   2. Artists' materials]
I. Shohet, Marti, ill.   II. Title   TT153.7.S27   1987   745.5'028   86-34271
ISBN 0-688-07374-3

to my family

Contents

Using This Book

There is fun and adventure in this book. With it, you can learn how to make your own materials for art projects. The most often used and asked for art and craft recipes are here. The book will save classroom teachers and leaders of troops, campers, clubs, and church and temple groups much money and effort because so many different recipes are compiled under one cover. When children learn to mix and make their own materials, many avenues of creative expression open up to them. Busy parents will find many useful rainy-day projects to both occupy and entertain children.

Most of the materials used in these recipes are inexpensive and are found in the home. A few items must be purchased in crafts stores or in pharmacies. In either case, the finished media will be less expensive than ready-made products. They will certainly be more rewarding.

The first thing you should do is read the Helpful Hints section and look through the entire book to become acquainted with the recipes. In many cases you will find several recipes for the same thing, such as paste, finger paint, and modeling compound. Some of these recipes are simple, some are more complicated. Each produces a medium with a unique texture or consistency. You will have fun experimenting with different recipes to determine which you prefer.

Most of the recipes are designed and measured for individual projects. Some recipes include instructions for increasing them for group work. Teachers, parents, and group leaders should determine which recipes are best suited for their particular needs.

Although an effort has been made to avoid the use of harmful ingredients, it is recommended that, when using these recipes, children be supervised to prevent accidents. It is also recommended that no one eat or taste any of the finished products. They are not for human consumption.

Helpful Hints

1. There are many preservatives for pastes, finger paints, and modeling compounds. You can use powdered alum, oil of cloves, oil of cinnamon, lemon extract or an antiseptic, such as Listerine or Bactine. In most cases only one or two of these preservatives are listed in the recipe, but you can substitute any from the above list. The preservatives suggested in this book are those most frequently found in the home, at a pharmacy, or in the health-aids section of a grocery store. These substances should not be eaten.

2. For the most part, coloring materials have been limited to poster paints, powdered pigments, dyes, food coloring, and zinc oxide because they are readily available and inexpensive. Zinc oxide powder is a paint pigment that is often used in antiseptic lotions. It can be purchased in a pharmacy.

3. Unless another kind of flour is specifically called for, always use plain non-self-rising wheat flour in all recipes calling for flour.

4. For successful results, all measurements should be followed carefully. Since ingredients may vary somewhat from brand to brand, you may have to experiment until you have found the correct quantities for a particular recipe.

5. Never pour leftover plaster or plaster mix down the drain. It will clog drainpipes.

6. A plastic coffee-can lid or similar plastic lid is a good base on which to make bowls or figures with modeling compounds. A lid can be easily turned so that you can work on all parts of the object, and you can easily carry it to another place for drying.

7. You may wish to purchase a palette pan for mixing paints.

8. Dextrine, which is used in some of these recipes, is easily obtainable in most groceries or drugstores. It is a powdered or granulated sugar substitute that usually contains saccharin, but this will not affect the recipe.

9. In several recipes, commercial white household glue—a casein glue—is suggested for expedience. When other glues can be substituted, they are mentioned.

10. All of the other ingredients used in this book can be purchased in a grocery store or drugstore except rosin, resin glue, plaster of Paris, and the chemicals needed for making colorful flames, pinecones, and fireplace logs; these items can be purchased at a lumberyard or hardware store.

PASTES
AND
GLUES

Thin Paste

You Will Need:

1/4 cup sugar
1/4 cup non-self-rising wheat flour
1/2 teaspoon powdered alum
1 3/4 cups water
1/4 teaspoon oil of cinnamon

How to Make It:

1. In a medium-sized pan, mix together sugar, flour, and alum.
2. Gradually add 1 cup water, stirring vigorously to break up lumps.
3. Boil until clear and smooth, stirring constantly.
4. Add remaining water and oil of cinnamon. Stir until thoroughly mixed.

Makes 1 pint.

How to Use It:

Spread paste with a brush or tongue depressor.

Thin Paste is an excellent adhesive for scrapbooks, collages, and Strip Papier-mâché (page 62).

This paste can be stored in a jar for several months without refrigeration.

Paper Paste

You Will Need:

⅓ cup non-self-rising wheat flour
2 tablespoons sugar
1 cup water
¼ teaspoon oil of cinnamon

How to Make It:

1. Mix flour and sugar in a saucepan. Gradually add water, stirring vigorously to break up lumps.
2. Cook over low heat until clear, stirring constantly.
3. Remove from stove and add oil of cinnamon. Stir until well blended.

Makes about 1 cup.

How to Use It:

Spread paste with a brush or tongue depressor.

Soft, smooth, thick, and white, Paper Paste has a good spreading consistency and is especially appropriate for use with small children or for any paste-up work.

This paste can be stored in a covered jar for several weeks without refrigeration.

Classroom Paste

You Will Need:

1 cup non-self-rising wheat flour
1 cup sugar
1 cup cold water
4 cups boiling water
1 tablespoon powdered alum
½ teaspoon oil of cinnamon (optional)

How to Make It:

1. Combine flour and sugar in a large pot. Slowly stir in cold water to form a paste.
2. Slowly add boiling water, stirring vigorously to break up lumps.
3. Bring mixture to a boil, stirring constantly, until thick and clear.
4. Remove from heat and add alum. Stir until well mixed.
5. Add oil of cinnamon if paste will not be used immediately.

Makes about 1½ quarts.

How to Use It:

Classroom paste is a good all-purpose paste, especially appropriate for work with children. It is also excellent for papier-mâché projects.

Stored in a closely capped jar, this paste will keep for several weeks. It keeps longer than Paper Paste (page 17) and is a little softer. If it gets too thick it can be thinned with hot water for easy spreading.

Japanese Rice Paste, a Transparent Library Paste

You Will Need:

¾ cup rice flour (can be purchased at health food store or
    diet food section in grocery)
2 tablespoons sugar
¾ cup cold water
2½ cups boiling water
½ teaspoon oil of cinnamon

How to Make It:

1. Mix rice flour, sugar, and cold water in a medium-size
pan. Stir until smooth.
2. Add boiling water.
3. Bring to boil over low heat, stirring constantly, until mixture thickens.
4. Remove from heat and add oil of cinnamon.

Makes 1½ pints.

How to Use It:

Japanese Rice Paste is excellent for mending torn pages of books. Cut a piece of white tissue paper the size and shape of the tear. Spread paste over the tissue and lay the tissue over the tear. The paste will be transparent when it dries.

You can use this paste for tissue-paper collages and scrapbooks. Spread with a brush or tongue depressor.

If stored in a tightly sealed jar, this paste will keep for several months without refrigeration.

Instant-Rice Paste

You Will Need:

¼ cup dry instant rice
1 cup water
  electric blender
¼ cup warm water
1 teaspoon of an antiseptic, such as Listerine or Bactine

How to Make It:

1. Put rice in a bowl. Pour in ½ cup water and let set overnight.
2. Pour into blender and add ¼ cup warm water. Liquify for five minutes. Do not undermix or paste will be lumpy.
3. Pour liquid mixture into a saucepan and add ½ cup water. Warm for five minutes, stirring constantly.
4. Remove from heat. Let cool. Add antiseptic to prevent spoilage.

Makes ½ cup.

How to Use It:

This thick paste dries clear and is a good base for finger paints. To make paints, just add food coloring or powdered pigments.
  Store the paste in a covered glass jar.

Liquid Rice Paste

You Will Need:

2 tablespoons instant rice
¾ cup warm water
    electric blender
    pinch of sodium benzoate or a few drops of antiseptic
        (such as Listerine or Bactine) to retard spoilage

Warning: Omit sodium benzoate if paste is to be used with young children.

How to Make It:

1. Put rice in a bowl and cover with warm water. Let set overnight.
2. Place mixture in blender and add sodium benzoate or antiseptic. Liquify 4 to 5 minutes.

Makes ½ cup.

How to Use It:

This paste is great for making tissue paper collages. It can be stored in a covered glass jar for several days without refrigeration.

Resin Papier-mâché Paste

You Will Need:

½ cup non-self-rising wheat flour
¼ cup powdered resin glue
½ cup warm water
1½ cups hot water
4 drops oil of cinnamon

How to Make It:

1. Mix flour and resin glue in a saucepan.
2. Make a paste by adding ½ cup of warm water. Add hot water, stirring vigorously to prevent lumps.
3. Cook over low heat, stirring constantly, until mixture is thick, clear, and smooth.
4. Add oil of cinnamon.

Makes about 1 pint.

How to Use It:

For best results, use this paste within a few days of preparation.

The paste gives a very hard finish to papier-mâché projects and is excellent for making large papier-mâché objects such as furniture, candlesticks, and bowls.

Store paste in a covered glass jar.

Wallpaper Paste

You Will Need:

4 cups non-self-rising wheat flour
1 cup sugar
1 gallon warm water
1 quart cold water
½ teaspoon oil of cinnamon (optional)

How to Make It:

1. Mix flour and sugar in a large pan.
2. Add enough warm water, a little at a time, to make a smooth paste. Then add the rest of the warm water slowly, stirring vigorously to break up lumps.
3. Bring mixture to a boil, stirring constantly. Cook until thick and clear.
4. Thin with about 1 quart cold water to desired consistency.
5. Add oil of cinnamon if paste will not be used the same day it is made.

Makes about 1½ gallons.

How to Use It:

This paste spreads best when used warm. It will keep for a few days.

This is a good paste to use for making Strip Papier-mâché (page 62) and other projects that require a large amount of paste. You can use it for covering lamp shades and wastebaskets with cloth or wallpaper if durability is not required.

Paperhanger's Paste

You Will Need:

  1 cup non-self-rising wheat flour
  1 tablespoon powdered alum
  1 tablespoon powdered rosin
1½ cups warm water
4½ cups hot water
1½ cups cold water
  8 drops oil of cloves or oil of cinnamon (optional)

How to Make It:

1. Mix flour, alum, and rosin in a large pot.
2. Make a paste by adding 1½ cups warm water. Stir until smooth.
3. Pour in 4½ cups hot water, stirring vigorously to break up lumps.
4. Place over low heat and boil until thick and clear.
5. Thin with about 1½ cups cold water.
6. Add 8 drops oil of cloves or cinnamon as preservative if paste will not be used the same day it is made.

Makes about 1½ quarts. Can be doubled for large projects.

How to Use It:

This paste is best when used warm. As it cools, it will thicken. It can be thinned with more warm water. If preservative is added, it will keep several months.

Paperhanger's Paste can be used for papier-mâché projects to obtain a hard finish. This paste makes a durable binding agent for gluing cloth on cardboard to reinforce box corners or for affixing scrapbook hinges.

24

Stamp Gum

You Will Need:

- 1 packet (¼ ounce) unflavored gelatin
- 1 tablespoon cold water
- 3 tablespoons boiling water
- ½ teaspoon white corn syrup
- ½ teaspoon lemon extract

How to Make It:

1. In a small bowl, sprinkle gelatin into cold water. Put aside until softened.
2. Pour softened gelatin into boiling water and stir until completely dissolved.
3. Add corn syrup and lemon extract. Mix well.

Makes 4 ounces.

How to Use It:

Brush gum thinly onto the back of a stamp. When dry, moisten the stamp and apply it to paper.

This gum will gel overnight. To return it to a liquid state, warm container of gum in a pan of hot water. If stored in a pill bottle, Stamp Gum will keep several months.

Seal and Envelope Mucilage

You Will Need:

6 tablespoons pure white vinegar
4 packets (1 ounce) unflavored gelatin
1 tablespoon lemon extract

How to Make It:

1. Bring vinegar to a boil in a small pan. Add gelatin and stir until completely dissolved.
2. Add lemon extract. Stir until well mixed.

Makes about ½ cup.

How to Use It:

Use a brush to spread mucilage thinly on the back of a label or an envelope flap. Let dry. Moisten to apply.

This is a thicker, heavier glue than Stamp Gum (page 25). You can use this mucilage to adhere paper to paper or to cardboard. Apply and stick at once.

With this mucilage and paper, you can make your own envelopes, note stationery, labels, and seals. The recipe provides enough mucilage for a large group to use. One-half cup of mucilage will cover several dozen envelopes or labels.

Store leftover mucilage in a capped bottle. It will keep for several months without spoiling. It will set when cooled, however. To use again, melt mucilage by putting the bottle in a pan of warm water.

Waterproof or Glass Glue

You Will Need:

2 packets (½ ounce) unflavored gelatin
2 tablespoons cold water
3 tablespoons skim milk
   several drops oil of cloves (optional)

How to Make It:

1. In a small bowl, sprinkle gelatin over cold water. Set aside to soften.
2. Heat milk to boiling point and pour into softened gelatin. Stir until gelatin is dissolved.
3. Add oil of cloves as preservative if glue is to be kept for more than a day.

Makes about ⅓ cup.

How to Use It:

While the glue is still warm, brush a thin layer on the objects to be glued.

This is the best glue to use for projects in which glass must be adhered to glass. For gluing decorations on glass jars, it is best to use the glue in its liquid state. For gluing marbles together or gluing metal ornaments to metal cans, use the glue in its gelled state. This glue is waterproof and can be used to mend china, to glue labels on home-canned foods and jellies, or to glue wood to wood.

Store glue in a screw-capped jar. It will gel as it cools, but this will not affect its adhesiveness. Set jar in a pan of hot water to soften glue for reuse.

Bookbinding or Leather Glue

You Will Need:

1 packet (¼ ounce) unflavored gelatin
3 tablespoons boiling water
1 tablespoon vinegar
1 teaspoon glycerine

How to Make It:

1. In a pan, add gelatin to boiling water. Stir until gelatin is completely dissolved.
2. Add vinegar and glycerine. Stir until well mixed.

Makes about ⅓ cup. For larger projects, double the recipe.

How to Use It:

While the glue is still warm, apply a thin layer with a brush.

This waterproof glue is excellent for binding leather to leather. It also makes a good flexible glue for use on paper, or for gluing cloth to cardboard for making notebook binders or scrapbooks.

Stored in a tightly capped plastic or glass jar, this glue will keep for several months. It will gel in the bottle after a few days. Warm bottle in hot water to reuse glue.

Collage or Découpage Glue

You Will Need:

3 parts white household glue*
1 part warm water

*A thin solution of Paperhanger's Paste (page 24) or Waterproof or Glass Glue (page 27) can be substituted.

How to Make It:

1. Combine glue with water in a jar or a bottle with a screw-top lid.
2. Shake until well mixed.

How to Use It:

To make a collage, brush a thin layer of glue to the back surface of paper scraps or pictures and smooth them onto a piece of cardboard.

For a découpage, start by cutting out a design and brushing a thin layer of glue to the back surface. Lay the design on the surface to be decorated and smooth out all air bubbles and wrinkles.

This glue may be stored indefinitely.

MODELING
COMPOUNDS

Preparing Natural Clay

You Will Need:

natural clay
1 two-pound coffee can
   old newspapers
   a hammer or a rock to be used
      as a hammer
   ¼-inch mesh sieve
2 three-pound coffee cans with lids
   water
   window-screen wire
   large plaster bowls or cloth-lined bowls

How to Make It:

Many areas of the country contain natural clay banks. These vary in color—gray, green, red, or yellow—depending upon the mineral found in combination with the clay. This natural clay can be used to make pottery or sculpture.

1. Select a clay deposit that is as free from impurities (sand, gravel, dirt, plant roots, and stems) as possible. Dig enough clay to fill a two-pound coffee can.

2. Spread out the clay on newspapers and place it in the sun to dry completely.

3. The clay will dry in hard lumps. With a hammer or rock, break these lumps into a fine powder, being careful not to crush pebbles or rock chips into the clay.

4. Sift the powdered clay through the sieve. Discard all pebbles.

5. Fill one three-pound coffee can ⅔ full with the sifted clay. Completely cover clay with water. As the water soaks into the clay, pour on more water so that the clay remains immersed.

32

6. Using your hands, stir the clay to evenly distribute the water throughout it.

7. Let the mixture soak for about 2 hours, or until it is the consistency of thick cream.

8. To break up lumps, pour mixture through a piece of window-screen wire into another coffee can or a bucket.

9. Let this strained mixture sit overnight, or until all the clay has settled to the bottom. Then pour off the clear water that has accumulated on top. Do not stir up the thick "slip" underneath.

10. Pour the remaining thick slip into large plaster bowls or bowls lined with dry cloths. Plaster bowls are best if you have them, but cloth-lined bowls are satisfactory. As the cloth absorbs the water, the slip stiffens and separates from the cloth or plaster. Store the slip, or moist clay, in covered coffee cans for several days. The clay improves with age. You should store it moist, since the clay will dry out when you cut and wedge it.

11. All clay must be "wedged" to remove air bubbles before it can be used. Cut the clay into pieces and throw each piece with force against a table many times until you are sure no more air bubbles remain. After this is done, your clay will be ready to use.

If the clay will not hold its shape, you can improve it by adding a little fine sand.

If the clay crumbles at the edges when you press it between your fingers, it is too sandy. If the clay is too sandy to work with, there is little that can be done to improve it. It is best to discard it and select another clay deposit. With a little experimentation and practice, you will soon learn which kind of natural clay suits you best.

Quick and Easy Modeling Dough

You Will Need:

¾ cup flour (use any kind except self-rising flour)
½ cup salt
1½ teaspoons powdered alum
1½ teaspoons vegetable oil
½ cup boiling water
   food coloring

How to Make It:

1. Combine flour, salt, and alum in a mixing bowl.
2. Add vegetable oil and boiling water. Stir vigorously with a spoon until well blended. Dough should not stick to the sides of the bowl and should be cool enough to handle.
3. Add food coloring and knead into dough until color is well blended and the dough is the desired tint.

Makes about 1 cup. Double the recipe for large projects. For groups, mix several double recipes rather than one large amount.

How to Use It:

This is an excellent play dough. It has a smooth texture, takes about 15 minutes to make, and dries to a hard finish overnight. Use it to make lovely dough flowers as well as animals and other figures.

Store in a jar with a tight lid. Dough will keep several months without refrigeration.

Play Clay

You Will Need:

½ cup salt
½ cup hot water
¼ cup cold water
½ cup cornstarch

How to Make It:

1. In a pan, mix salt and hot water and heat to boiling point.
2. Stir cold water into cornstarch in a small bowl.
3. Add cornstarch mixture to boiling water. Stir vigorously to break up lumps.
4. Cook over low heat, stirring constantly, until mixture is like stiff pie dough.
5. Remove from heat and turn out onto a breadboard to cool.
6. As soon as mixture is cool enough to handle, knead until smooth and pliable.

Makes about 1½ cups.

How to Use It:

Play Clay has a grainy texture and is excellent for flattening with a rolling pin and cutting into shapes to make mobiles and holiday decorations.

It dries and hardens in 1 to 2 days. When dry, it is white and can be painted with enamels. To speed up drying time, bake on a cookie sheet in an oven at 200 degrees Fahrenheit for 1 hour.

Wrapped in aluminum foil or plastic or stored in an airtight container, the clay will keep a long time without refrigeration.

Cooked Salt-and-Flour Clay

You Will Need:

¾ cup salt
¾ cup non-self-rising flour
 2 teaspoons powdered alum
¾ cup water
 2 tablespoons vegetable oil
   food coloring

How to Make It:

1. Mix salt, ½ cup flour, and alum in a saucepan.
2. Add water slowly, stirring to break up lumps.
3. Place over low heat and cook, stirring constantly, until mixture is rubbery and difficult to stir. It should not be sticky when touched.
4. Add vegetable oil. Stir until blended.
5. Turn out onto a plate or aluminum foil. Set aside until cool enough to handle.
6. If more than one color is desired, divide mixture into portions and to each portion add a different food coloring. Knead until color is blended.
7. Add up to ¼ cup flour if clay is sticky.

Makes 1½ cups.

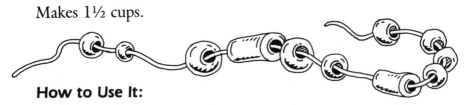

How to Use It:

Model as with any clay. Press clay into molds or use it to make beads. (Pierce holes in beads before clay dries.)

This clay hardens in 1 or 2 days; do not bake. Store in an airtight container.

Play Dough

You Will Need:

2¼ cups non-self-rising wheat flour
  1 cup salt
  1 tablespoon powdered alum
  4 tablespoons vegetable oil
1½ cups boiling water
    food coloring or poster paints

How to Make It:

1. Combine flour, salt, and alum in a bowl. Add vegetable oil.
2. Stir in boiling water. Stir vigorously with a large spoon until mixture holds together.
3. Knead the dough until it is smooth.
4. Divide the dough into several lumps. Add a few drops of food coloring or poster paint to each lump and knead to mix the color into the dough.

Makes about 3 cups.

How to Use It:

Model as with any clay. Objects will dry to a hard finish if left in the open air. Paint dried pieces with enamel, hyplar, or tempera.

Stored in an airtight container, Play Dough will keep a long time.

Creative Play Clay

You Will Need:

1 cup baking soda
½ cup cornstarch
⅔ cup warm water
    food coloring or poster paints
    shellac or clear nail polish

Completed project

How to Make It:

1. Mix baking soda and cornstarch in a saucepan.
2. Add water. Stir until smooth.
3. Place over medium heat and bring to a boil. Cook, stirring constantly, until mixture looks like mashed potatoes.
4. Remove from heat and pour onto mixing board to cool.
5. When clay is cool enough to be easily handled, knead.
6. For color, knead food coloring into the clay until well blended, or paint finished, uncolored objects with poster paints.
7. When pieces are completely dry, brush with shellac or clear nail polish. Shellac is optional for figures colored with food coloring.

Makes about 1½ cups. Double the recipe for large groups or for large objects.

How to Use It:

With a rolling pin and cookie cutters or a knife, you can roll and cut out Creative Play Clay to make holiday ornaments, mobiles, and three-dimensional pieces.

This mixture can also be molded into almost anything—flowers, animals, birds. It hardens quickly, so work with only

38

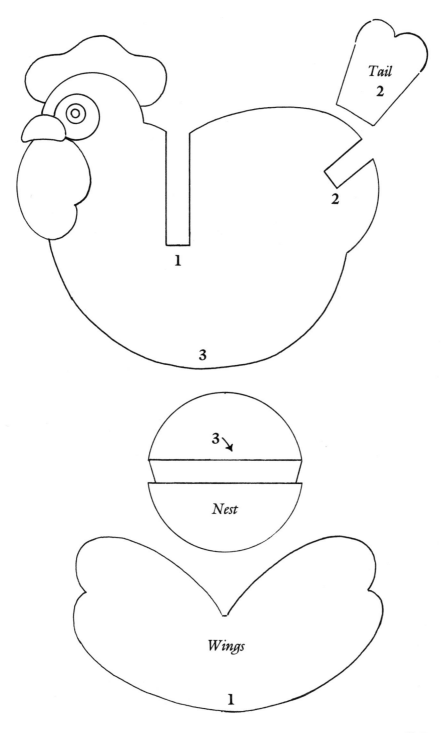

Tail
2

2

1

3

3

Nest

Wings

1

39

a small amount at a time. The larger the object, the longer it will take to dry.

Stored in plastic bags or in airtight containers, this clay will keep several weeks.

CLAY PATTERN

Trace pattern onto cardboard. Cut out.

Roll clay ¼ inch thick. Lay pattern pieces on clay and cut around with sharp knife.

To assemble, fit pieces into numbered slots. Set in slot in "nest." Let dry.

Flour Modeling Dough

You Will Need:

1 cup salt
1½ cups hot water
4 cups flour

How to Make It:

1. Put salt in a bowl and add hot water.
2. Stir until salt is dissolved.
3. Add flour and stir until thoroughly mixed.
4. Knead until mixture is soft and spongy.
5. Place in a plastic container or storage bag and let set for several hours.

Makes about 4 cups.

How to Use It:

This dough is soft and pliable, and easy to use. Start by preheating oven to 300 degrees Fahrenheit. Shape dough into any object you desire. Do not make the object too thick or it will not bake properly. Dough can also be rolled out and cut with a cookie cutter.

Bake objects on a cookie sheet for about 1 hour. Let cool, then paint with watercolors or tempera. Spray with clear varnish or plastic fixative. Finished pieces may be glued together.

Extra dough will keep for a week or more in an airtight container in the refrigerator.

Brown Bread
Modeling Dough

You Will Need:

½ cup plain salt
¾ cup hot water
2 cups whole-wheat flour
1 tablespoon vegetable oil

How to Make It:

1. In a bowl, dissolve the salt in the water. Add flour and oil.
2. Mix with your hands. Knead until well blended, keeping hands wet.

Makes about 2 cups.

How to Use It:

Mold dough into desired shapes, or roll out and cut designs with cookie cutters.

Bake on foil-lined cookie sheet at 300 degrees Fahrenheit for about 1 hour or until dry.

This is an excellent dough for modeling holiday decorations, jewelry, and plaques.

Salt Modeling Clay

You Will Need:

> 1 cup non-self-rising wheat flour
> ½ cup salt
> 1 teaspoon powdered alum
> ⅓ to ½ cup water
> food coloring (optional)
> model enamel (optional)

How to Make It:

1. Combine flour, salt, and alum in a bowl.
2. Add water a little at a time, and stir into the flour mixture until it is like pie dough.
3. Knead until dough is thoroughly mixed and has a smooth consistency.
4. This clay is white. It can be left this way and the finished articles can be painted with model enamel. Or, food coloring can be added and kneaded into the moist clay until well blended. The clay can also be divided into portions and a different food coloring can be added to each portion.

Makes about 1½ cups. Double recipe for large groups.

How to Use It:

Model as with any clay, or roll clay ½ inch thick and cut shapes with a cookie cutter. Make designs by pressing a nail file or similar instrument into the clay. For details, add clay, wetting the underside to make it stick to the basic piece.

This clay is excellent for making Christmas tree ornaments. Glue on a loop of string for hanging when clay dries, or make a small hole for string while ornament is wet.

Within 2 to 3 days, Salt Modeling Clay dries to a hard surface. For quick drying, bake on a cookie sheet 1 to 2 hours, depending on the size of the article, at 200 degrees Fahrenheit.

Stored in a plastic bag in an airtight container, this clay will keep a long time.

Sand and Cornstarch Modeling Dough

You Will Need:

1 cup sand
½ cup cornstarch
1 teaspoon powdered alum
¾ cup hot water
    food coloring (optional)

How to Make It:

1. Mix sand, cornstarch, and alum in a bowl.
2. Add hot water, stirring vigorously until well mixed.
3. Add food coloring, if desired, and blend.
4. Cook over medium heat until thick, stirring constantly.

Makes about 2 cups.

How to Use It:

When sufficiently cooled, mold dough into objects. Dry pieces in the sunshine for several days.

This modeling dough is grainy and stonelike; it can be used to make interesting sculptures. It does not need shellac or varnish for protection.

Store leftover dough in an airtight container.

Sawdust Modeling Compound

You Will Need:

1 cup fine sawdust
   food coloring (optional)
   old newspapers
1 cup Thin Paste (page 16) or Paper Paste (page 17)
   shellac or clear varnish (optional)

How to Make It:

1. To obtain a colored compound, mix sawdust with food coloring in a glass jar. Drain and spread on newspapers to dry before using.
2. Mix sawdust and paste to a thick doughlike consistency. Knead until thoroughly mixed. The amount of paste required may vary with the kind of sawdust used. If the sawdust is coarse, more paste may be needed to obtain a doughlike consistency.

Makes about 1 cup.

How to Use It:

Model as with any clay. Bits of dough may be added to the basic piece by moistening and sticking them down.

Within two to three days, the finished article will harden. To speed up drying, bake at 200 degrees Fahrenheit for 1 to 2 hours, depending on the size of the article. To give the article a permanent finish, spray with shellac or varnish.

Articles molded from this compound have a lovely woodgrain appearance. They can also be sanded to give a smoother finish.

Soapsuds Clay

You Will Need:

¾ cup soap powder, such as Ivory Snow
1 tablespoon warm water
electric mixer

How to Make It:

1. Mix soap powder and water in a large bowl.
2. Beat with an electric mixer to a claylike consistency.

Makes about 1 cup. The recipe may be doubled or tripled for larger objects. Be sure to use the same proportions.

How to Use It:

Mold clay into figures and other objects. The clay dries to a hard finish.

To make simulated snow: Beat 2 parts soap powder to 1 part water and spread like icing on a piece of heavy cardboard. This "icing" may also be used to decorate cardboard holiday ornaments. It dries to a smooth, rubbery surface overnight.

Dryer-Lint Modeling Material

You Will Need:

3 cups dryer lint
2 cups cold or warm water
⅔ cup non-self-rising wheat flour
3 drops oil of cloves
    old newspapers

How to Make It:

1. Put lint and water in a large saucepan. Stir to dampen all of the lint.
2. Add flour and stir thoroughly to prevent lumps.
3. Add oil of cloves.

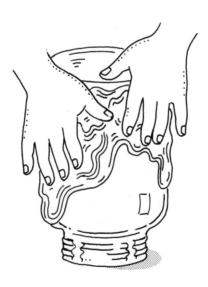

4. Cook over low heat, stirring constantly, until mixture holds together and forms peaks.

5. Pour out and cool on several thicknesses of newspaper.

Makes about 4 cups.

How to Use It:

Shape over armatures (boxes, bottles, balloons, and so forth), press into a mold, or use as you would papier-mâché pulp.

This material will dry in 3 to 5 days to a very hard, durable surface. When wet, it has a feltlike consistency. It dries smooth or rough, depending on how it is used. Press material into a mold to obtain a hard, smooth finish.

Stored in an airtight container, this material will keep for several days.

Salt Map Mixture Number One

You Will Need:

1 part salt
1 part non-self-rising wheat flour
2/3 part water
    food coloring or poster paints
    heavy cardboard

How to Make It:

1. In a bowl, mix salt and flour until thoroughly blended.
2. Add just enough water to make mixture the consistency of a thick icing. The more water you use, the longer the mixture will take to dry.
3. Stir thoroughly.
4. Add food coloring to mixture before molding, or mold and paint when dry.

How to Use It:

Draw a map on heavy cardboard. Spread mixture on cardboard, shaping appropriate hills and valleys. This is also an excellent mixture for making three-dimensional projects such as box dioramas.

This mixture will dry in 1 to 2 days, depending on how thickly it is spread. The longer the mixture takes to dry, the more likely your cardboard is to warp. The thinner the layer of mixture, the lighter-weight the cardboard can be.

A contour map will keep indefinitely.

Salt Map Mixture Number Two

You Will Need:

2 parts salt
1 part non-self-rising wheat flour
1 part water
   food coloring or poster paints
   heavy cardboard

How to Make It:

1. Mix salt and flour in a large bowl.
2. Add water a little at a time until the mixture reaches the consistency of icing. Stir thoroughly.
3. Add food coloring to small amounts of the mixture and stir until each color is well blended, or paint the surface of the dried mixture with poster paint.

How to Use It:

Mixture should be used at once. On heavy cardboard, spread mixture as you would to ice a cake. Build up high elevations a little at a time by allowing the first layer to dry before adding the second layer. Mixture will take 1 to 3 days to dry, depending on its thickness.

This mixture has a whiter, grainier texture than Salt Map Mixture Number One (page 50) and dries to a harder surface, but it takes longer to dry. The hardened surface keeps indefinitely.

Bread Dough Clay

You Will Need:

1 slice white bread
1 teaspoon white glue
1 tablespoon water
    food coloring
    clear glaze or clear nail polish

How to Make It:

1. Cut or tear crusts from bread. Discard crusts.
2. Pour glue, then water, onto the center of the slice of bread.
3. Knead until dough doesn't stick to your fingers.
4. Divide dough into several parts and add a few drops of food coloring to each. Knead until color is well blended.
5. Place each color in a separate plastic bag.

Makes enough clay for several small objects.

How to Use It:

Work with only a small portion of clay at a time. Shape objects and allow them to dry overnight. When dry, spray with clear glaze or paint with clear nail polish.

Bread Dough Clay can be stored in the refrigerator for several days.

Bread Modeling Dough

You Will Need:

2 slices day-old white bread
2 tablespoons white household glue
2 drops glycerine
4 drops white vinegar
   food coloring or poster paint

How to Make It:

1. Cut or tear crusts from bread. Discard crusts.
2. Break bread into small pieces in a bowl.
3. Add glue, glycerine, and vinegar.
4. Mix dough with your hands. Knead until it no longer sticks to your fingers and until it is smooth and pliable. (It will be sticky at first, but will soon become doughlike.)
5. Divide the dough and add a few drops of coloring to each portion. Knead until the color is smoothly blended.

Makes enough dough for two or three small objects.

How to Use It:

To prevent the dough from sticking to your hands, use lotion when modeling. Do not try to make large pieces or the dough will crack when drying.

This dough is excellent for making jewelry; flowers; doll heads, hands, and feet; and for decorating boxes, frames, and other objects.

Allow pieces to dry 1 to 2 days. Objects made with this dough dry slowly, but have a smooth satiny finish. A porcelainlike finish can be obtained by painting pieces with 2 or 3 coats of a mixture of 1 tablespoon of white glue and 1 table-spoon of water. Allow each coat to dry before applying the next. A ceramiclike finish can be obtained by baking the glue-coated objects at 225 degrees Fahrenheit for 4 minutes.

Stored in a plastic bag in the refrigerator, Bread Modeling Dough will keep a long time.

Rose Petal Bread Dough

You Will Need:

⅓ cup non-self-rising wheat flour
1 tablespoon salt
2 tablespoons water
3 cups rose petals
   round toothpicks

How to Make It:

1. In a bowl, mix flour and salt with water to make a stiff dough.
2. Cut rose petals into tiny pieces, then crush by rolling them between your palms.
3. Mix as many rose petals into your dough as possible without making it crumbly.
4. Shape small amounts of dough into beads.
5. Push round toothpicks through the center of each bead to make holes.
6. If desired, scratch rose petal designs into beads.
7. Allow to dry a few days. Remove toothpicks before dough gets too hard.

Makes enough beads for 1 necklace.

How to Use It:

String beads on cord after they are thoroughly dry.

Gesso Modeling Dough

You Will Need:

1 teaspoon Sobo or other good-grade white household glue
1 tablespoon dextrine solution (1 cup powdered dextrine
    dissolved in 1 tablespoon hot water)
¼ cup plaster of Paris, patching plaster, whiting, Bon Ami,
    unscented talcum, or powdered chalk
    palette knife or putty knife
    model enamel, or tempera and shellac

How to Make It:

1. Pour Sobo onto a plate.
2. Add dextrine solution and mix well.
3. Add plaster of Paris 1 tablespoonful at a time. Mix with
a palette knife or putty knife until plaster will not absorb any
more solution and can no longer be mixed.
4. Scrape dough together and knead it, using plaster to keep
it from sticking to your hands. Knead several minutes, adding more plaster until you have a pliable claylike mixture that
is stiff enough to hold its shape. Mix two batches for larger
projects.

Makes enough dough for two or three small objects. Mix
two batches for larger projects.

How to Use It:

Working with a small amount of dough, model small objects such as flowers and ornaments for attaching to picture
frames, boxes, three-dimensional plaques, and so forth. To
make an agent for fastening pieces together or to a base, mix
a few drops of dextrine solution with a few drops of glue
and a little plaster.

Set aside to dry for at least a week before painting. To paint, use model enamel or tempera. Apply a coat of shellac over tempera.

Dough made with one of the materials other than plaster can be stored indefinitely if kept moist with a damp cloth in an airtight container.

Gesso Painting Paste

You Will Need:

1 teaspoon white household glue
1 tablespoon dextrine solution (1 cup powdered dextrine
    dissolved in 1 tablespoon hot water)
  patching plaster or powdered chalk
  oil-paint brush, waxed-paper cone, or cake decorator
  small sharp knife
  oil paints or enamels

How to Make It:

1. Mix glue with dextrine solution in a small bowl.
2. Add just enough patching plaster to make a paste thick enough to hold its shape but soft enough to apply with an oil-paint brush.

Makes enough gesso for one small project.

How to Use It:

Draw a pattern or design on whatever you are decorating (furniture, boxes, beads, picture frames, and so forth). Fill in the design with the gesso until the desired height is attained. This may be done with an oil-paint brush, a waxed-paper cone, or a cake decorator. If you plan to raise the design fairly high, raise it only a third at a time, allowing each stage to dry before applying the next. The gesso can also be shaped and carved with a small sharp knife.

    Gesso is excellent for repairing antique picture frames or

furniture. Objects to be mended must be free of dirt, grease, or paint. When gesso is dry, paint with oil paints or enamels.

You can also use gesso to form letters of the alphabet or other designs on waxed paper. When hardened, glue designs to another surface.

Nutty Putty

You Will Need:

1 tablespoon liquid starch
2 tablespoons white glue (such as Elmer's School Glue)
3 drops food coloring (optional)
   pinch of sodium benzoate to retard mold (optional)
   plastic Easter egg or small screw-top jar

Warning: Omit sodium benzoate if material is to be used with young children.

Makes about 3 tablespoonsful.

How to Make It:

1. Measure starch into a small bowl. Add glue. Let set five minutes.
2. If desired, add coloring and sodium benzoate. Then mix thoroughly until all starch is absorbed and color is spread smoothly throughout. The more you mix the putty, the better it gets.
3. Store in a plastic Easter egg or small jar.

How to Use It:

This recipe makes a rubbery putty that will bounce, pick up pictures from the newspaper, stretch, and mold into shapes. If left in the open air, it will melt into a rubbery blob and turn hard. If a tougher, more rubbery putty is desired, add one more teaspoonful of starch. Soft putty should set overnight before being used to pick up pictures. If used too soon, it may stick to the paper.

Stored in an airtight container, Nutty Putty will last several days. If the surface dries out or if it gets too tough from handling, just dip it into warm water and then knead.

PAPIER-MÂCHÉ

Strip Papier-mâché

You Will Need:

old newspapers
Thin Paste (page 16), Resin Papier-mâché Paste (page 22),
  or Wallpaper Paste (page 23)

How to Make It:

1. Tear newspapers into long thin strips from the fold down. For large objects, tear the strips 1 to 1½ inches wide. For small objects, tear narrower strips.
2. If paste is thick, thin with water for easy spreading.
3. Lay paper strips on a sheet of newspaper and cover one side of the strips with paste. Strips may also be pulled through paste, but they will take longer to dry. Or paste can be applied to an armature and the dry strips laid over the paste.

How to Use It:

Strip Papier-mâché is a good material for making small animals, puppets, piñatas, masks, and other articles.

Cover a base or armature (a balloon, a rolled newspaper frame, a jar, a light bulb) with strips of paste-covered newspaper running in one direction. Apply a second layer of strips in the same manner, running these strips perpendicular to the first layer. Continue this way until you have built up 4 or 5 layers. To help you determine when you have completely covered the base with each layer, use the colored comic sections for alternate layers.

Allow 1 to 2 days for drying.

Pasted Paper Layers
Papier-mâché

You Will Need:

old newspapers
Thin Paste (page 16), Paper Paste (page 17), or Paperhanger's Paste (page 24)

How to Make It:

1. Cut newspaper into pieces slightly larger than your intended finished project.
2. Spread a piece of newspaper liberally with paste and lay a second piece over it. Cover the second piece with paste and lay another over it. Continue in this way until you have built up a strong thick pad. The number of layers you need will be determined by the size of the object you are making. Beginners can start with 6 or 8 layers for small objects such as jewelry; add more layers for larger objects.

How to Use It:

This papier-mâché is an excellent material for making flowers.

Draw the outline of your design on the top sheet of paper and cut it out while the layers of papier-mâché are still damp. Shape and set aside to dry for 1 to 2 days.

Very large pieces, such as those used on parade floats, can also be made if they are strengthened with a layer of cloth. Tear the cloth the same size as the newspaper pieces. Spread paste on cloth. Use the cloth as a middle layer; cover with other newspaper sections.

Basic Papier-mâché Pulp

You Will Need:

newspaper
pail
1 pail or large pan warm water
electric mixer
thick Classroom Paste (page 18), Resin Papier-mâché Paste
   (page 22), or Wallpaper Paste (page 23)
oil of cloves
poster paints
shellac

How to Make It:

1. Tear newspaper into 1-inch-wide strips or into pieces measuring 1 x 1½ inches. Tear enough to fill pail.

2. Sprinkle strips into water, stirring to separate them until all have been added. If necessary, add more water until all the paper is covered. Set aside overnight.

3. Beat soaked paper with an electric mixer until you have a smooth pulp.

4. Strain out excess water. Squeeze pulp with hands until nearly dry.

5. Add paste gradually. The amount you need depends upon how much paper pulp you have and how dry you have squeezed the pulp. Mix to a claylike consistency with an electric mixer or with your hands.

6. Add a few drops of oil of cloves to prevent mold from forming while drying.

How to Use It:

Shape or model as with clay. Place the finished object in a spot where the air can circulate around it until it is completely dry. Allow 3 to 5 days to dry, depending on the size of the object. If the object cracks while drying, mend it with additional pulp.

Paint the object with poster paints and then shellac.

Variation: For interesting and different textures, mix sawdust or sand with the pulp. More paste is required in these mixtures.

Salt Papier-mâché

You Will Need:

    old newspapers
    water
    large pan or bucket
    electric mixer
 3 parts pulp
 1 part non-self-rising wheat flour
⅓ part salt
    oil of cloves
    poster or tempera paints
    lacquer or shellac

How to Make It:

1. Tear newspaper into pieces 1 x 1½ inches. Gradually add paper to a large pan or bucket of water, stirring until each piece is wet. Set aside overnight.

2. With an electric mixer, beat newspaper pieces to a smooth pulp.

3. Drain excess water and squeeze pulp until just moist. Do not squeeze dry.

4. Mix flour and salt together in a bowl and add to pulp. With an electric mixer, mix until smooth and claylike. If you find that the pulp is too moist, add more flour.

5. Add a few drops of oil of cloves to prevent mold from forming while drying.

How to Use It:

Model as with clay or build up object on an armature. Allow 3 to 5 days to dry, depending on the size of the object. Paint with poster or tempera paints. To waterproof the surface, cover with lacquer. If waterproofing is not necessary, cover with shellac.

Large Figure or Float Papier-mâché

You Will Need:

old newspapers
2 gallons warm water
　small tub or 3-gallon pail
　electric mixer
3 quarts pulp
1 pint paste (any kind)
2 cups plaster of Paris
　poster or tempera paints
　clear varnish or lacquer

How to Make It:

1. Tear newspaper into long strips.
2. Drop a few strips at a time into the small tub of warm water, stirring to ensure that all pieces are separated.
3. Set aside overnight.
4. Pour off part of the water and beat the paper pieces to a smooth pulp with an electric mixer or with your hands. To mix with your hands, squeeze the mixture through your fingers again and again. Continually stir up the mixture so that all parts become smooth and claylike. Rub stubborn pieces between thumb and fingers to break them up.
5. Add paste and plaster of Paris. Beat mixture with electric mixer or blend with your hands until smooth and claylike.

Makes enough papier-mâché for 1 fairly large object or several small objects. For larger objects, mix more than one batch at a time.

How to Use It:

Spread mixture over chicken wire, boxes, or rolled or crumpled newspaper frames. Model as with clay but work quickly, because the plaster of Paris makes this papier-mâché set faster and harder than ordinary papier-mâché.

Allow piece 3 to 5 days to dry thoroughly. Paint with poster or tempera paints. Waterproof with clear varnish or lacquer.

Papier-mâché Mash

You Will Need:

2-quart bowl or pan
old newspapers
½ gallon water
1 large enamel or aluminum pot or bucket
slotted spoon
electric mixer
collander or wire strainer
1 cup non-self-rising wheat flour
4 drops oil of cinnamon
poster or tempera paints
sandpaper
shellac or varnish

How to Make It:

1. Fill bowl with newspaper strips torn into pieces ½ x 1½ inches.
2. Place water in large pot and bring to a boil.
3. Add newspaper pieces, a few at a time, to the boiling water, stirring constantly with slotted spoon to separate them.
4. Cook over medium heat about 20 minutes, or until the paper fibers are broken down. Stir occasionally.
5. Beat with electric mixer until smooth.
6. Pour into collander to strain out excess water, but do not squeeze. Return paper to pot.
7. Add flour, mix well, and return strained mixture to heat.
8. Cook at low heat until stiff enough to stand in piles.
9. Add oil of cinnamon and mix.
10. Pour mash onto a thick pad of newspapers to cool.

Makes enough mash for 1 fairly large object or several small objects. To make large objects, such as furniture, quadruple the recipe. In place of the 2-quart bowl, use a second bucket.

How to Use It:

In cooking Papier-mâché Mash, the paper pulp is broken down into a softer, smoother consistency than can be achieved with Basic Papier-mâché Pulp (page 65). The mash dries to a very hard, durable finish. The finished article can be sanded smooth.

Model as with clay. Cover jars and bottles to make candlestick holders and vases. To make stools, bookshelves, and end tables, cover each side of a cardboard box with a layer of mash ½ inch thick.

Allow several days to dry. To speed drying, bake at 200 degrees Fahrenheit. The length of baking time required depends on the size of the article. Check the article frequently to test for dryness.

When dry, sand the article to a smooth finish and paint with poster or tempera paints. Then shellac or varnish.

Stored in the refrigerator, Papier-mâché Mash will keep a long time.

Extra Soft Papier-mâché Pulp

You Will Need:

paper napkins, facial tissues, or toilet tissue
Thin Paste (page 16) or white household glue

How to Make It:

1. Crumple napkins or tissue and cover with paste.
2. Model to desired shape.

How to Use It:

This pulp is an especially good material for adding details such as noses, ears, and eyebrows to larger pieces.

It does not keep and must be used immediately.

Finishing Touches to Papier-mâché Articles

1. To achieve a harder, more permanent, and waterproof surface, brush small papier-mâché articles with a coat of raw linseed oil. Then bake at 250 degrees Fahrenheit until dry.

2. To waterproof larger articles, brush on (do not spray) lacquer or clear waterproof varnish.

3. Shellac gives a good permanent finish, but it is not waterproof.

4. Liquid epoxy gives great strength and is flexible, but it should not be used by children working alone.

CASTING
COMPOUNDS

Mock Marble

You Will Need:

 2 teaspoons white glue
½ cup water
    plaster of Paris
    tempera paint (green, blue, gray, or any marble color you
       prefer)
    mold suitable for plaster casting

How to Make It:

1. Mix glue and water in a medium-size bowl.
2. Stir in enough plaster of Paris to make a thick frostinglike mixture.
3. Pour the mixture into a shallow soup bowl.
4. Pour a fairly thick coat of tempera paint over the top of the mixture.
5. Fold in the color to produce streaks. Do not blend.
6. Pour the mixture into a mold.

Makes about 1 cup. For large molds, double or triple the recipe.

How to Use It:

   Mock Marble can be used with any plastic or rubber molds suitable for plaster casting. These molds can be purchased at craft or hobby stores.
   Mock Marble produces an interesting, more durable variation on ordinary plaster of Paris.

Imitation Alabaster

You Will Need:

2 parts plaster of Paris
1 part water
    mold suitable for plaster casting
    pure white wax or paraffin
    tin can
    fine thread or wire

How to Make It:

1. Mix plaster of Paris and water in a bowl. Stir until smooth and creamy.

2. Pour into a mold. Set aside until plaster hardens.

3. Cut wax into small pieces and put in a tin can. Set can in a pan of hot water over a low flame to melt wax. Wax should be thoroughly melted and hot. Do not omit putting can in a pan of water. It is very dangerous to melt wax over a direct flame.

4. Remove object from mold. Tie a piece of fine thread around object and warm it in an oven at approximately 100 degrees Fahrenheit.

5. Holding the warm object by the string, dip it into the melted wax. Continue dipping until plaster of Paris absorbs as much wax as possible.

6. Hang up article to dry.

7. Remove string and polish object with a damp cloth.

How to Use It:

Imitation Alabaster can be used with any plastic or rubber molds suitable for plaster casting. These molds can be purchased at craft or hobby stores. The sheets of plastic bubbles that are used to package hardware items make interesting molds for paperweights or free-form statues.

Extra Strong Plaster of Paris (For Casting)

You Will Need:

2 parts plaster of Paris
1 part water
1 tablespoon white household glue for each ¼ cup water
    mold suitable for plaster casting

How to Make It:

1. Measure plaster into a bowl.
2. Mix water and glue in a separate bowl.
3. Pour water and glue mixture over plaster and stir until smooth and creamy. When preparing large amounts, it is better to pour the plaster into the water instead of the water over the plaster.

How to Use It:

Pour mixture into any plaster-casting mold. Set aside until it hardens. This mixture will dry hard and smooth.

Plaster of Paris Mixture for Dipping Cloth

You Will Need:

1½ parts plaster of Paris
  1 teaspoon powdered alum for each cup water
  1 part water
    cloth, gauze, paper towels, or old sheeting

How to Make It:

1. Mix plaster of Paris and alum.
2. Add plaster and alum mixture to water.
3. Stir until smooth and creamy.

How to Use It:

Dip cloth into plaster mixture. Drape the cloth over a bottle, a cardboard cone, wire, or whatever you are using for an armature. You will have 15 to 20 minutes to drape and shape the cloth before it dries. It will dry very hard.

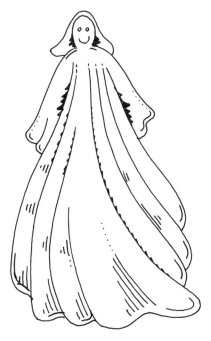

Slow-Drying Dipping Mixture

You Will Need:

1 gallon milk carton for mixing
1½ cups water
1 cup spackle compound
1 cup plaster of Paris
1 teaspoon powdered alum
slotted spoon
poster paint (optional)
cloth, gauze, paper towels, or old sheeting

How to Make It:

1. Cut top off milk carton. Pour water into carton.
2. In a bowl, mix together spackle, plaster of Paris, and alum.
3. Sprinkle mixture into water, allowing it to pile up in the center.
4. Stir with a slotted spoon until smooth and creamy.
5. Add poster paint if desired.

How to Use It:

Dip cloth into mixture, then drape and shape it around a bottle, armature, or other object. Since this mixture requires 45 minutes to set, you have plenty of time to mold or to correct mistakes.

This is a good mixture to use for making large parade-float figures over a base of chicken wire.

The recipe can be doubled, but for large objects it is better to mix 2 smaller amounts to prevent the mixture from setting before you have finished.

PAINTS
AND
PAINT MEDIUMS

Finger Paint Number One

You Will Need:

½ cup non-self-rising wheat flour
2 cups water
1 tablespoon glycerine
1 teaspoon borax for preservative
   small screw-top jars
   food coloring or poster paints

Warning: Borax can be toxic if swallowed. If this paint is to be used with small children, omit borax and mix only enough paint to use at one time or substitute another preservative.

How to Make It:

1. In a saucepan, mix flour with ½ cup of water to form a paste.
2. Add the rest of the water and cook over low heat until thick and clear, stirring constantly.
3. Let cool. Add glycerine and borax. If mixture is too thick and does not spread easily, thin with a small amount of water.
4. Divide and pour into small screw-top jars. Add food coloring or poster paints to tint.

Makes about 2 cups. For a large group of children, double the recipe.

How to Use It:

Dip shelf paper or typing paper into water and spread smoothly on a washable tabletop or on newspapers. Add a dab of finger paint and make a picture or a design. To spread finger paint evenly, dip your hands in water.

This finger paint spreads easily and thinly. It is flexible and does not crack or peel from paper that is folded. The paint works as well on dry paper as it does on wet paper, but with dry paper there is less curl.

Stored in airtight containers, this finger paint will keep a long time.

Finger Paint Number Two

You Will Need:

½ cup cornstarch
¾ cup cold water
2 cups hot water
2 teaspoons Listerine for preservative
1 tablespoon glycerine
  small screw-top jars
  food coloring or poster paints

How to Make It:

1. In a saucepan, mix cornstarch with ¼ cup of cold water to make a smooth paste.
2. Add hot water, stirring vigorously to prevent lumps.
3. Cook over low heat, stirring constantly, until mixture begins to boil.
4. Remove from heat and add ½ cup cold water and Listerine. Stir until thoroughly mixed.
5. Add glycerine to mixture to slow up drying process.
6. Pour mixture into separate screw-top jars and add food coloring or poster paints for color. Stir until color is completely blended.

Makes about 2½ cups. For a large group, double the recipe.

How to Use It:

Because it dries slowly, this is an excellent finger paint to use with small children. It has a smoother, glossier finish and is more transparent than Finger Paint Number One (page

82). It works as well on dry paper, which will have less curl, as it does on wet paper.

Stored in airtight containers, this finger paint will keep a long time.

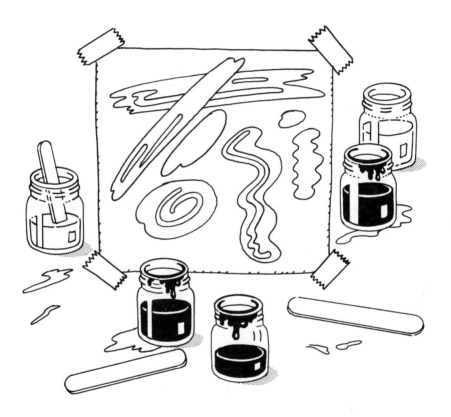

Finger Paint Number Three

You Will Need:

¼ cup laundry starch
¼ cup cold water
1½ cups boiling water
2 tablespoons talcum powder, preferably unscented
¼ cup soap powder, such as Ivory Snow
½ teaspoon Bactine
4 screw-top jars
1 tablespoon poster paint or ¾ tablespoon powdered tempera or several drops food coloring for each drop of finger paint

How to Make It:

1. In a saucepan, mix starch with cold water to make a smooth paste.
2. Add boiling water, stirring vigorously to break up lumps.
3. Cook over low heat until clear and thick, stirring constantly.
4. Remove from stove and add talcum powder. Stir until blended.
5. Add soap powder and Bactine. Mix until thoroughly blended.
6. Pour into four ½-cup screw-top jars (baby food jars are ideal).
7. Add coloring to each jar. Allow to cool.

Makes 2 cups. For large groups, double the recipe.

How to Use It:

This paint is thick and works best on wet paper. It has a flat finish and is more opaque than Finger Paints Number One (page 82) and Number Two (page 84).

In tightly capped jars, this paint can be stored for a long time.

Finger Paint Number Four

You Will Need:

½ cup cornstarch
1 cup cold water
1 envelope unflavored gelatin
2 cups boiling water
small screw-top jars
food coloring or poster paints

How to Make It:

1. In a saucepan, mix cornstarch with ¾ cup of cold water to a smooth paste.
2. Soak gelatin in ¼ cup of cold water. Set aside until ready to use.
3. Pour boiling water slowly into the cornstarch mixture, stirring as you pour.
4. Cook over medium heat, stirring constantly, until mixture boils and clears.
5. Remove from heat. Stir in gelatin.
6. Cool and divide into separate jars. Stir a different food coloring or poster paint into each jar until well blended.

Makes about 2½ cups.

How to Use It:

This paint is transparent and has a strong, durable, high-gloss finish. Use it on wet or dry paper. It is excellent paint for covering boxes, scrapbooks, and so on. It dries more quickly than Finger Paint Number Two (page 84).
If refrigerated, it will keep a few days.

Bathroom Finger Paint

You Will Need:

¼ cup non-abrasive household cleanser (such as Bon Ami)
paper cup
water
2 or 3 drops food coloring

How to Make It:

1. Pour cleanser into a paper cup.
2. Add enough water to make a thick paste.
3. Add food coloring and mix thoroughly.

Makes ¼ cup.

How to Use It:

Give paint to a child to play with in the bathtub. This paint is great for making artistic creations on the shower walls and sides of tub. Paint washes off easily, taking bathtub ring with it.

Simple Egg Tempera Emulsion

You Will Need:

2 measures of egg yolk
1 measure of water
   assorted powdered pigments or poster colors
   palette pan
   paint brush

How to Make It:

1. Since egg yolks vary in size, break up yolks in a measuring cup. Then determine the measure of egg yolk to determine the amount of water needed. The relation is 2 to 1. For example, if you have 2 tablespoons of egg yolk, you will need 1 tablespoon of water.
2. Mix egg yolks and water thoroughly until well blended. Do not beat.
3. In a palette pan, combine a small amount of the egg mixture with each powdered pigment. Work with a clean brush until thoroughly mixed.

Two egg yolks make about ¼ cup. For large groups, mix any measure of yolk with half as much water.

How to Use It:

This emulsion is a permanent paint with an opaque finish. One color can be painted over another. Mix only as much as you will be using at one time.

This emulsion is water soluble. Use water to thin emulsion and to clean brushes.

Stored in an airtight jar in the refrigerator, the base emulsion will keep for several days.

Egg Tempera Emulsion

You Will Need:

>   1 tablespoon dammar varnish (available at art supply or
>   craft stores)
>   8-ounce screw-top bottle or jar
>   1 whole medium-sized egg
>   1 tablespoon raw linseed oil
>   3-4 tablespoons water (depending on how thick or thin you
>   want your emulsion)
>   powdered pigments

Warning: This emulsion should not be swallowed.

How to Make It:

1. Pour a small amount of dammar varnish into a clean bottle. Shake to coat all sides; pour out excess varnish.
2. Break the egg into the bottle and shake until the yolk and the white are thoroughly mixed.
3. Add linseed oil and remaining dammar varnish and shake again until thoroughly blended.
4. Add the water and shake again until well blended.

Makes about ½ cup.

How to Use It:

When you are ready to use it, mix this emulsion with powdered pigments. Use water or base emulsion to thin.

Egg Tempera Emulsion is more brittle than oil paint and may crack when applied in thick layers. When it is used on canvas, panel, or good watercolor paper, attractive paintings can be produced. It dries waterproof with a mat finish.

Clean brushes immediately with soap and water.

Store in a tightly capped jar in the refrigerator.

Old-Fashioned Gouache Paint Medium

You Will Need:

 5 ounces gum arabic or gum tragacanth
 ½ cup distilled water
   pint jar with a lid
 ½ cup honey
 1 tablespoon glycerine
   powdered pigment or poster paints

How to Make It:

1. Dissolve the gum arabic in distilled water in a pint jar.
2. Mix in honey and glycerine.
3. Stir or shake until thoroughly blended.

Makes about 1½ cups.

How to Use It:

When you are ready to use it, mix this gouache base with powdered pigments or poster paints in a palette pan. Muffin tins make good pans for mixing pigments with gouache.

Gouache, which is opaque, can be used on illustration board or heavy drawing paper just like oil paints.

Zinc oxide mixed with gouache base makes a good white pigment.

Gouache is an interesting medium to work with and makes an inexpensive base for teaching young beginning painters. It has the advantage of being water soluble so that clean-up time is easier. Use water to thin gouache and to clean your brushes.

Stored in an airtight jar, gouache will keep for several months.

Gouache Paint Medium

You Will Need:

2 cups dextrine
   pint jar with a top
4 tablespoons distilled water
½ cup honey
2 teaspoons glycerine
½ teaspoon boric acid solution
   tempera or poster paints

Warning: Boric acid can be toxic if swallowed. Omit if small children will be using the mixture.

How to Make It:

1. Pour dextrine into a pint jar.
2. Add water and stir until dextrine is dissolved. The saccharin in the dextrine will cause the mixture to foam; this does not matter.
3. Add honey, glycerine, and boric acid solution.
4. Stir or shake until all ingredients are well blended.

Makes about ¾ cup.

How to Use It:

When you are ready to use it, mix this gouache base with tempera or poster paints. It is opaque and dries rapidly. One color can be painted over another. This gouache medium is a good substitute for Old-Fashioned Gouache Paint Medium (page 93) if you cannot obtain gum arabic.

Use water to thin medium and to clean your brushes.

Stored in a tightly capped jar, Gouache Paint Medium will keep for a long time.

Gouache Paint

You Will Need:

2 cups dextrine
  pint jar with a lid
4 tablespoons distilled water
2 tablespoons glycerine
½ teaspoon boric acid solution
  powdered pigments
  zinc oxide
  flat plate
  palette knife
  small screw-top jars

Warning: If you plan to use this paint with small children, omit the boric acid solution. It can be toxic if enough is swallowed.

How to Make It:

GOUACHE BASE

1. Pour dextrine into a pint jar. Add distilled water and stir until dextrine is completely dissolved. The saccharin in the dextrine will cause the mixture to foam; this does not matter.
2. Add glycerine and boric acid solution.
3. Put lid on jar and shake until thoroughly blended.

Makes slightly more than ½ cup.

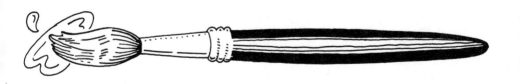

GOUACHE PAINT

1. Pour 1 or 2 tablespoons of one powdered pigment and an equal amount of zinc oxide onto a flat plate. Mix thoroughly with a palette knife.

2. Add enough gouache base to make paint a soft butterlike consistency. Mix thoroughly with palette knife until smooth.

3. Lift paint with palette knife and transfer to screw-top jars.

How to Use It:

Gouache Paint is opaque, dries rapidly, is water soluble, and has a flat finish. It will become a darker color when it dries. Use it on paper, poster board, illustration board, or any surface you would paint with watercolors. Mix larger amounts for painting large objects, such as stage backdrops or murals.

Clean your brushes with water.

Gouache Paint can be thinned with water or with uncolored gouache base.

Stored in a tightly capped jar, this paint will keep for several weeks.

Mucilage Gouache Paint Medium

You Will Need:

½ cup gum mucilage
½ cup strained honey
   ½-pint jar with a lid
   powdered pigments or poster paints
   zinc oxide, if desired (see Helpful Hints, Number 2 on
     page 12)

How to Make It:

1. Mix mucilage and honey in a ½-pint jar.
2. Shake until smoothly blended.

Makes about 1 cup.

How to Use It:

Mix this medium with powdered pigments or poster paints when you are ready to use it. Use zinc oxide for white pigment. This medium dries slowly.

Use water to thin medium and to clean your brushes.

Stored in a tightly capped jar, this medium will keep for several months.

Casein Paint Medium

You Will Need:

2 tablespoons borax
½ cup warm water
¼ cup powdered nonfat milk
   powdered pigments

Warning: This paint medium should not be swallowed.

How to Make It:

1. In a bowl, dissolve borax in warm water.
2. Add powdered milk. Stir until completely blended. Mixture should be a thick, creamy solution.

Makes about ¾ cup. For a larger group, double the mixture.

How to Use It:

Combine only as much medium with colors as you intend to use at one sitting. In a palette pan, use a brush to mix small amounts of the medium with powdered pigments to the consistency of thick cream.

Casein Paint Medium dries quickly to a semigloss finish. One color can be painted over another.

Use water to thin medium and to clean your brushes.

Stored in a screw-top jar in the refrigerator, this medium will keep several weeks.

Casein Paint

You Will Need:

2 parts casein glue (white household glue)
1 part water
   powdered pigments, poster paints, or opaque watercolors

How to Make It:

1. Mix glue and water.
2. Combine mixture with powdered pigment. Mix until paint is the consistency of thick cream.

How to Use It:

Casein Paint, which has a flat finish, is especially good for painting on waxed surfaces such as the sides of milk cartons and cottage cheese cartons. Use Casein Paint when you want a more permanent finish than can be obtained with tempera or poster paints.

Use water to thin paint and to clean your brushes.

Store this paint in a tightly capped jar.

Powdered-Milk Paint Medium

You Will Need:

½ cup powdered nonfat milk
½ cup water
   powdered paint pigments

How to Make It:

1. Mix milk and water in a bowl. Stir until milk is dissolved.
2. Combine only as much solution with powdered pigments as you intend to use at one sitting.

Makes about ¾ cup. For a large group, combine any amount of powdered milk with an equal amount of water.

How to Use It:

In a palette pan, mix small amounts of the solution with powdered pigments. Work smooth with a brush.

This paint dries quickly to a glossy, opaque finish. It does not dust, chip, or come off on your hands like poster paint.

Use water to thin paint and to clean your brushes.

Store medium in a tightly capped jar in the refrigerator.

Milk Poster Paint

You Will Need:

¼ cup powdered paint pigment
¼ cup powdered milk
 2 teaspoons cornstarch
½ cup warm water

How to Make It:

1. Mix all dry ingredients together.
2. While stirring, gradually add water. Continue to stir until paint is smooth and creamy.

Makes slightly less than 1 cup.

How to Use It:

This smooth, opaque paint is excellent for painting stage scenery, murals, posters, or on waxed surfaces such as milk cartons.

The recipe can be halved or doubled, but it is best to mix only as much paint as you will need at a time. Mix colors in jars or plastic spray-can lids.

This paint can be kept overnight if stored in closed containers. Or pour leftover paint into paint cups and allow to dry. Then use with a wet brush just like any watercolor paint.

Silk Screen or Poster Paint

You Will Need:

2 parts powdered pigment
1 part liquid starch

How to Make It:

1. Mix pigment and starch thoroughly until smooth and creamy.

How to Use It:

This paint bonds better than pigments mixed with water and will cover a greater variety of surfaces. It is excellent for silk-screening designs on paper.

Store in capped paint jars.

Watercolors

You Will Need:

1 tablespoon white vinegar
2 tablespoons baking soda
1 tablespoon cornstarch
¼ teaspoon glycerine
    plastic bottle caps or paint pans
    red, yellow, and blue food coloring

How to Make It:

1. Mix vinegar and baking soda together in a small bowl.
2. When mixture stops foaming, add cornstarch and glycerine. Mix well.
3. Pour mixture into plastic bottle caps or paint pans.
4. Add several drops of a different food coloring to each pan. Stir until the color is well mixed. The tint may look lighter when dry, so be sure to add plenty of coloring. To make green, add equal amounts of blue and yellow; for orange, equal amounts of red and yellow; for purple, equal amounts of blue and red; for brown, 1 drop of blue, 1 drop of red, and 2 drops of yellow. Paint will be liquid at this stage.
5. Let set overnight to harden.

How to Use It:

This paint makes a good substitute for regular boxed watercolors, especially in an emergency. However, it tends to be slightly powdery when dry.

Marbleizing

You Will Need:

8 packets (2 ounces) unflavored gelatin
1 pint boiling water
   shallow baking pan
5 pints cold water
   oil paints
   turpentine
   brown wrapping paper or paper bags

Warning: Do not use turpentine with small children.

How to Make It:

1. Dissolve gelatin in boiling water.
2. Pour mixture into shallow pan and add cold water.
3. In separate bowls, mix each oil paint with a bit of turpentine to the consistency of thick cream.
4. Drop a few spots of one color into solution in shallow pan. If the color sinks, the solution is too thick. If color spreads too much, it is too thin. When the solution is just right, drop in large spots of each color, one at a time.
5. With a spoon or stick, swirl into patterns.

How to Use It:

Cut a piece of brown paper to the size of the pan. Hold the paper by opposite corners and lower onto the solution. Lift paper carefully and lay right side up on newspapers to dry.

Marbleized paper can be used for covering scrapbooks, notebooks, lamp shades, wastebaskets, and many other objects.

Clean pan with turpentine.

Homemade Coloring for Paints and Modeling Clays

You Will Need:

beets or cranberries
onion skins
spinach
cornflower petals or blueberries
instant coffee
water (use rainwater or distilled water for all colors)
glass or enamel saucepan
glass jars
sodium benzoate

Warning: Sodium benzoate can be toxic if swallowed. Omit if coloring is to be used with young children.

How to Make It:

1. For red coloring, cut beets into small parts and put into saucepan. Cover with cool water. Cook over medium heat for 30 minutes. Remove and let set until cool. Strain juice into a glass jar.

Or add one cup of water to cranberries and boil in an uncovered pan. Cook for 15 minutes. Let cool, then strain juice into a clean jar.

2. For yellow, place onion skins in saucepan and cover with water. Boil for 30 minutes. When cool, pour juice into glass jar.

3. For green, place spinach leaves in saucepan and cover with water. Boil 30 minutes. When cool, strain into jar.

4. For blue, pick cornflowers at peak of color. Cut petals into small pieces and put in saucepan. Cover with water. Boil for 15 minutes. Cool, strain out flowers, and save the juice in a glass jar. Or boil blueberries for 15 minutes. Cool and strain juice into glass jar.

5. For brown, dissolve 1 teaspoon of instant coffee in 2 tablespoons of hot water. Let cool.

How to Use It:

Mix dye with paint medium or clay base.

To preserve dyes, add a pinch of sodium benzoate to liquid and seal in airtight containers. Coloring will stay fresh for several months.

These liquid dyes can be kept for long periods by freezing. Let thaw for several hours before using.

Frescoes

You Will Need:

wooden picture frame (a narrow frame is preferable)
piece of ⅛-inch plywood to fit inside the frame (any thin
  board may be used)
plaster (patching plaster can be used)
water
paints that won't be injured by lime in the plaster (watercolors, poster paints, or tempera)
cardboard, hammer, and tacks

How to Make It:

1. Cut the plywood to fit inside the back of the frame. Use
hammer and tacks to secure in place *(see* A *on page 110)*.
2. Mix plaster according to instructions on package. Pour
out and cover the plywood on the frame side with about ¼
inch of plaster *(see* B*)*.
3. Use the edge of a piece of cardboard like a trowel to
smooth the surface of the plaster *(see* C*)*.
4. Let plaster set until almost dry but still damp.

How to Use It:

   While plaster is still damp, paint a design or picture on it.
Use either freehand or stencil designs. As the plaster contin-
ues to dry, the pigment sets in the plaster *(see* D*)*.
   To determine if paint is limeproof, mix a small amount of
the paint with dry plaster. If no change takes place in the
color after a week or so, the paint can be used.

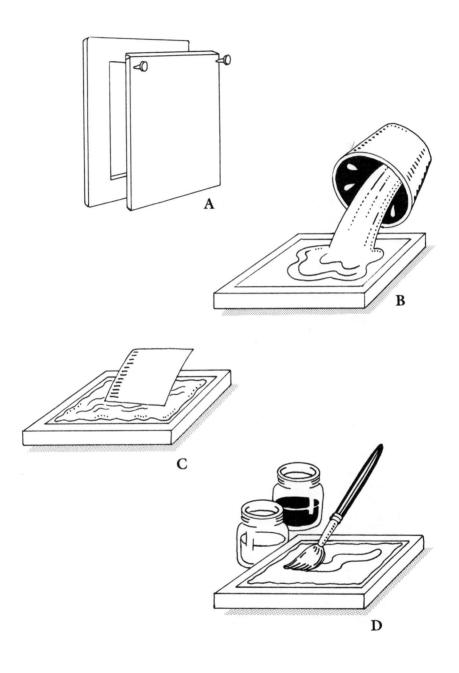

A

B

C

D

Oil Pastel Crayons

You Will Need:

1 ounce paraffin or candle wax
   clean empty can
1 teaspoon linseed oil or turpentine
3 tablespoons powdered paint pigment
   paper towel tube

Warning: Do not use turpentine with small children.

How to Make It:

1. Cut up paraffin or wax and place in a clean empty can. Set the can in a pan of water and place over low heat until wax is melted. Remove pan from heat.
2. Add linseed oil or turpentine. Stir until well mixed.
3. Now add powdered pigment. Stir well.
4. Pour a small portion of the mixture into a 3-inch section of a waxed paper roll or a paper towel roll. When hardened, add rest of mixture. Repeat for each color desired.

How to Use It:

When the mixture hardens, the tube may be removed from the entire crayon or from the tip only. Draw as with any crayon. Six-ounce frozen juice cans or similar tubelike cardboard containers may also be used as molds.

Oil Paint Medium for Thinning and Glazing

You Will Need:

1 ounce stand oil
1 ounce dammar varnish
5 ounces turpentine
15 drops cobalt drier

Warning: This mixture can be toxic if swallowed and should be kept out of reach of small children.

How to Make It:

1. Mix all ingredients together in a jar.

Makes 2½ ounces.

How to Use It:

To thin oil pigments, dip a brush into medium and mix with pigments on a palette. To glaze, brush medium over finished painting after paint is thoroughly dry.

INKS

· · · · · · · · · · · ·

Transfer Ink

You Will Need:

2 tablespoons soap powder, such as Ivory Snow (not a detergent) or scrapings from a bar of soap
¼ cup hot water
1 tablespoon turpentine

Warning: Turpentine can be toxic if swallowed. Keep out of reach of small children.

How to Make It:

1. In a bowl, dissolve soap powder in hot water.
2. Add turpentine.
3. When cool, pour into a screw-top bottle.

Makes about ¾ cup.

How to Use It:

Dip a watercolor brush into the ink and brush ink over the picture to be transferred. Wait about 10 seconds. Place a piece of paper over the picture and rub the back of it with a spoon. The picture will soon be transferred to the paper.

You can transfer an entire picture or just a portion of it by inking only the parts you wish to transfer. Comic strip characters transfer especially well. Magazine pictures will also work, but slick papers require a bit more ink. A picture can usually be transferred more than once.

You can use Transfer Ink to make stationery, greeting cards, and composite pictures. You can take a picture from a magazine for a school report, transfer wallpaper designs onto lamp shades, or designs onto shirts. The possibilities are unlimited.

Transfer Ink may be stored indefinitely without refrigeration. If the ink solidifies, set the bottle in a pan of warm water until the ink becomes liquid again. Shake well before using.

Block Printing Ink

You Will Need:

sheet of glass
3 tablespoons powdered pigment
1 tablespoon clear varnish
palette knife
brayer

How to Make It:

1. On a glass surface, mix pigment and varnish thoroughly with a palette knife.
2. Roll brayer back and forth until the mixture is tacky and the brayer is evenly coated.

Makes enough ink for 1 project. For large groups, double or triple the recipe.

How to Use It:

When the brayer is evenly coated, roll it over a carved wood or linoleum block. Press the block on paper and apply weight evenly.

To make potato or spool prints, press a carved potato or spool into the ink on the glass and then print on paper.

Block Printing Ink for Fabric

You Will Need:

5 tablespoons turpentine
2 tablespoons vinegar
1 tablespoon oil of cloves
1 tablespoon Ivory dishwashing liquid
   8-ounce bottle
   oil paint pigments
   palette knife
   sheet of glass
   brayer
   carved wood or linoleum block
   piece of fabric
   hot iron

Warning: Keep the ink out of reach of small children.

How to Make It:

1. Pour first four ingredients into bottle and shake well.
2. Thin oil paint pigments with this solution to the consistency of thick cream. On a piece of glass, work smooth with a palette knife.
3. Roll brayer back and forth until mixture is tacky and the brayer is evenly coated.

Makes enough ink for one project.

How to Use It:

When brayer is evenly coated, roll it over the carved block. Press the block over the fabric and apply weight evenly. Remove the block and place a damp cloth over the designed fabric. Press with a hot iron.

The designed fabric can be washed in warm water with a mild soap.

Waterproof Ink

You Will Need:

1 tablespoon powdered clothes dye (more may be added for deeper color)
2 teaspoons peppermint extract
1 tablespoon glycerine
¾ cup distilled water

Warning: Keep clothes dye and ink out of reach of children.

How to Make It:

1. In a small bowl, dissolve dye in extract.
2. Mix with glycerine.
3. Dissolve mixture in distilled water.

Makes about ¾ cup.

How to Use It:

Waterproof Ink can be used to stencil or paint fabrics, to make laundry marks, and so on.

Store this ink in a screw-top bottle.

Hectograph Ink

You Will Need:

1½ teaspoons water-based pigment, such as Prussian blue, iodine-green, or methyl violet (Do not use an oil paint pigment. Aniline dye is best but poisonous.)
1 teaspoon glycerine
4 teaspoons distilled water
⅔ teaspoon peppermint or lemon extract

Warning: Keep the ink out of reach of small children.

How to Make It:

1. In a small bowl or jar, mix the pigment with glycerine until smooth and well blended.
2. Add water and extract. Stir or shake until thoroughly mixed.

Makes about 2 tablespoons—enough for several projects.

How to Use It:

Store ink in a tightly capped bottle. Shake bottle well before using.

On typing paper, draw or write with a lettering pen or a fine brush. Make reprints on a hectograph pad, a kind of duplicator with a gelatin pad. You can make one (page 121) or buy one.

Hectograph Pad, a Duplicating Pad

You Will Need:

2 cups water
4 packets (1 ounce) unflavored gelatin
   baking pan, about 8 x 11 inches
2 teaspoons boric acid solution

Warning: Boric acid solution can be toxic to small children. Keep it out of their reach.

How to Make It:

1. In a bowl, pour water over gelatin and let stand for 2 to 3 hours *(see A on page 122)*.
2. Pour softened gelatin into baking pan.
3. Slowly bring to a boil, then reduce heat and let simmer over low heat for 20 minutes *(see B)*. Add boric acid solution.
4. Set aside overnight.

How to Use It:

A Hectograph Pad is used to make duplicate copies of letters or pictures. First write a letter or draw on typing or similar paper with Hectograph Ink (page 120), hectograph pencils, or copy pencils. Gently sponge the surface of the gelatin pad in the baking pan *(see C)*. The pad should be wet, but there should not be any puddles of water. Place the letter or drawing on the pad, face down, and rub out all wrinkles *(see D)*. Wait one minute, then remove the master sheet. You can now make copies from the pad. Lay a clean sheet of paper over the gelatin pad. Smooth paper by rubbing out wrinkles. Remove immediately. You can make many copies in this manner. When you are finished, wash the pad with a sponge and cold water. After the pad dries for a day, it will be ready for reuse.

If the pad dries out from lack of use, cover the top of the gelatin with warm water. Let stand for a few minutes, or until it no longer feels dry when sponged.

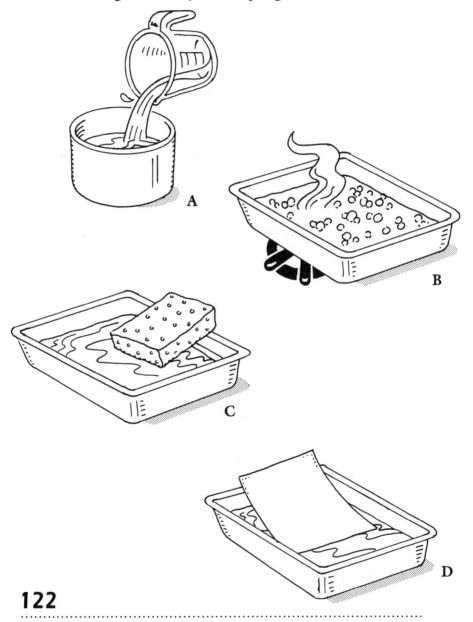

A

B

C

D

FLOWER
PRESERVATIVES

Flower Preservative with Cornmeal

You Will Need:

1 part powdered borax
2 parts cornmeal
  covered cardboard box (a shoe box or stationery box)
  fresh flowers

Warning: Keep borax out of reach of small children.

How to Make It:

1. Thoroughly mix borax and cornmeal.
2. Cover the bottom of the box with ¾ of an inch of the mixture.
3. Cut flower stems to about 1 inch long. Lay the flowers face down in the mixture. Spread the petals and leaves so that they lie as flat as possible. Do not place flowers too close together.
4. Cover the flowers with ¾ of an inch of mixture.
5. Place lid on box and keep at room temperature for 3 to 4 weeks.

How to Use It:

Using this method, try preserving daisies, pansies, apple blossoms, asters, violets, and other flowers. They will stay summer fresh indefinitely. This is an excellent way to preserve corsages or flowers from someone special.

Flower Preservative with Borax

You Will Need:

fresh flowers (roses, pansies, violets, sweet peas, chrysanthe-
  mums, zinnias, marigolds, and daisies)
florist's wire
airtight container (coffee can or plastic cottage cheese container)
plastic bag
borax
wire or string
soft brush

Warning: Keep borax out of reach of small children.

How to Make It:

1. Pick flowers at the peak of their bloom.
2. Remove stems. Make new stems with florist's wire. Run
wire through the base of each flower and twist the two ends
together.
3. Line the coffee can or plastic cottage cheese container with
the plastic bag.
4. Pour enough borax into the plastic bag to cover the bottom to a depth of 1 inch.
5. Place a flower face down in the borax. Pour about 1 inch
of borax over the top of the flower. Add more flowers and
borax until the container is full.
6. Gather the top of the bag, squeezing out all the air inside
it. Fasten shut with wire or string.
7. Place lid on can and set aside in a dry place for at least 4
weeks.

125

8. Remove flowers from borax and carefully brush away all borax with a soft brush.

How to Use It:

Twisting the wire stems, make an attractive flower arrangement as you would a fresh-flower bouquet. Flowers preserved in this way make colorful permanent arrangements. Flowers picked at the peak of their bloom remain fresh looking indefinitely.

Flower Preservative with Sand

You Will Need:

baking pan, 9½ x 13½ x 2 inches
3 quarts of sterile, dry, fine sand (Fine white sand can be purchased, but any clean light-colored sand can be used if it is first baked at 212 degrees Fahrenheit for 20 minutes and sifted through a fine screen.)
fresh flowers
flour sifter or wire sieve
paper towels
soft brush

How to Make It:

1. Fill the pan 1 inch deep with sand.
2. Place flowers face up on the sand.
3. Sift about 1 inch of sand over the flowers, carefully pushing sand under flowers so that they do not dry distorted.
4. Bake at 200 degrees Fahrenheit for about 2 hours. You might need to experiment a little to get the exact baking time for your flowers. To test, pour a little sand off one corner. If the flowers are still damp and droopy, they need to bake a little longer. If they are dull and dark, they baked too long. They should look about the same as they did when you put them in the oven.
5. Pour off the top layer of sand and carefully remove the flowers. Lay them on a paper towel to cool for an hour or so.
6. With a soft brush, carefully clean off all the sand that remains on the flowers.

How to Use It:

Flowers preserved by this method are excellent for making picture arrangements. Glue them to velvet or cardboard and then frame the picture.

To store flowers until you are ready to use them in a project, place them face down in cardboard boxes. The flowers will stay fresh looking for a long time.

MISCELLANEOUS

Fixative

You Will Need:

1 part pure white shellac
  screw-top glass jar
1 part denatured alcohol
  atomizer or spray gun

Warning: Keep fixative out of reach of small children.

How to Make It:

1. Pour shellac into jar.
2. Add alcohol.
3. Screw cap on tightly and shake until well blended.
4. Pour fixative into an atomizer or spray gun.

How to Use It:

To prevent charcoal, chalk, pastel, and pencil drawings from smudging, spray fixative on artwork from a distance of about 20 inches.

Crayon Cloth Design

You Will Need:

cloth
lightweight paper
crayons
iron
drawing board
thumbtacks
newspapers
½ cup vinegar
1 cup water
cloth for pressing
3 tablespoons salt
1 quart water

How to Make It:

1. Wash cloth to remove all sizing (stiffeners).
2. Stencil, draw, or transfer a design directly onto the cloth. To make a transfer pattern, draw a design on lightweight paper, then outline it with a sharp-pointed red or orange crayon. Lay the paper design face down on the cloth. Run a medium hot iron over the back of the paper to transfer the design onto the cloth.
3. Stretch the cloth smoothly and tightly over the drawing board. Thumbtack securely in place.
4. Color in your design with crayons, using an even, regular stroke. The more crayon you add, the deeper the color will be.
5. Remove cloth from drawing board. Turn the color design face down on several sheets of newspaper.
6. In a bowl, mix vinegar and 1 cup water. Dip pressing cloth into vinegar mixture and squeeze out most of the fluid.

131

Place the pressing cloth over the designed cloth and press with a hot iron.

7. Mix salt and 1 quart water in a bowl. Soak the designed cloth in this solution for 3 to 4 hours.

8. Gently wash cloth in lukewarm water and mild soap. When it dries, your design will be permanent. The cloth can be laundered in warm water and mild soap.

How to Use It:

The Crayon Cloth Design method can be used to decorate dishcloths, tablecloths, curtains, and so on.

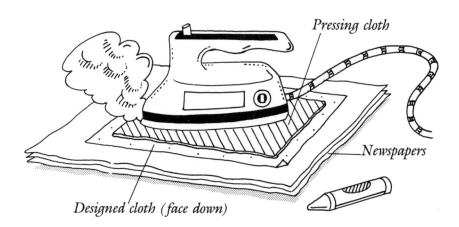

Pressing cloth

Newspapers

Designed cloth (face down)

Gesso Ground for Scratchboard

You Will Need:

1 part glue water (1 ounce gelatin to 16 ounces hot water)
1 part zinc white
1 part plaster of Paris
   illustration board

How to Make It:

1. Mix gelatin and water to make glue water. Set aside to cool.
2. Mix glue water with zinc white and plaster of Paris.
3. Stir until completely smooth and free of all grains.
4. Paint onto illustration board.
5. Let dry overnight.

How to Use It:

Brush over Gesso Ground with paint or black ink. Scratch a design or picture in the painted gesso with a needle, a nail, or other sharp instrument.

This gesso cannot be stored. Mix only as much as you will need for one project.

Crepe Paper Raffia

You Will Need:

strips of crepe paper, 2 to 3 inches wide (use crepe paper
    streamers or cut streamers from the end of a package)
spool or thumbtack and hand drill
clear spray varnish or shellac

How to Make It:

1. Thread one end of the crepe paper through the hole in the spool.
2. Twist and pull the entire length of crepe paper through the spool.
Or:
1. Fasten down one end of crepe paper with a thumbtack.
2. Fasten the other end to a hand drill.
3. Twist until paper is firm and cordlike.

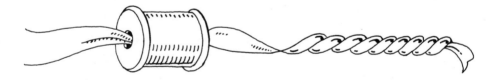

How to Use It:

One strip of raffia will be more than enough to cover a juice can, which you can use as a pencil holder. Wrap other containers in raffia to make attractive wastebaskets, sewing baskets, and May baskets.

Coat finished product with clear spray varnish or shellac.

Colored Flame Solution

You Will Need:

1½ pounds rock salt

½ gallon water

2 pounds of one of the following chemicals: calcium chloride (orange flame), potassium chloride (purple), copper chloride (blue), strontium nitrate (red), copper sulphate (emerald green), or lithium chloride (carmine)

small plastic tub or dishpan

stacks of old newspapers and heavy string; or pinecones or wood chips and mesh bag

Warning: Keep chemicals and flame solution out of reach of children and pets.

How to Make It:

1. Mix salt, water, and one of the chemicals in the plastic tub *(see A on page 136)*.

2. Fold several sheets of newspaper in half and roll into compact logs.

3. Using heavy string, tie logs securely, but not too tightly, because they will swell when they soak *(see B)*.

4. Soak the logs in the chemical solution for 3 weeks *(see C)*. Turn them frequently.

5. Remove logs from solution and let dry completely before burning. This can take a week or more, depending upon how damp the air is.

To treat pinecones or wood chips:

1. Place cones or chips in a mesh bag, such as a plastic onion or potato bag.

2. Mix 1 pound of a chemical in 1 gallon of water in a plastic tub.

3. Submerge the bag of cones or chips in the solution and weight it down with a brick or stone to prevent it from floating.

4. Soak for 10 to 15 minutes.

5. Pour out onto newspapers to dry overnight.

How to Use It:

When you burn these "logs" in your fireplace, each chemical produces a different colored flame.

Double or triple the recipe to make large quantities of logs or pinecones.

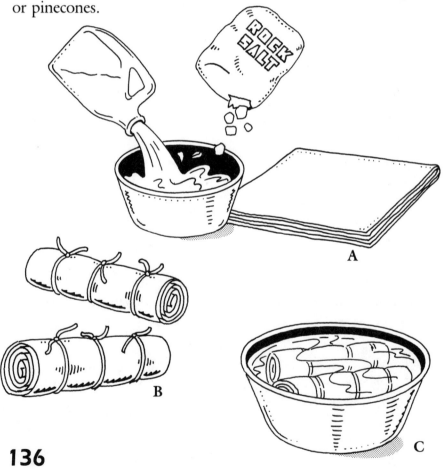

A

B

C

Fireplace Log Solution

You Will Need:

    stacks of old newspapers
    tuna cans or wire
½ gallon water
    plastic tub or dishpan
2 tablespoons lime
2 tablespoons vinegar
2 tablespoons salt substitute
1 tablespoon bluestone (copper sulfate)

Warning: Keep this solution out of reach of small children and pets.

How to Make It:

1. Fold newspapers in half, making a stack 1 inch high for each log, and roll as tightly as possible into logs.
2. Slip each log into a tuna can that has both ends cut out, or fasten log with wire. Do not tie with string. The string will burn and might allow pieces of newspaper to go up the chimney.
3. Pour water into tub.
4. In a bowl, mix the lime and vinegar. Add to water.
5. Then add salt substitute and bluestone.
6. Soak the rolls of newspaper in the solution for 3 to 4 weeks.
7. Dry logs thoroughly before storing. This will take several days, depending upon the weather or climate.

How to Use It:

    These logs will burn with a green flame.

Colorful Burning Pinecones

You Will Need:

1½ gallons hot water

  3 plastic or ceramic containers, one for each color

  ½ pound copper sulfate (for green flame)

  ½ pound boric acid (for crimson flame)

  ½ pound calcium chloride (for yellow or yellow-orange flame)

    pinecones

Warning: Keep the solution out of the reach of small children and pets. The chemicals can be toxic.

How to Make It:

1. Pour ½ gallon of hot water into each container.
2. Add one chemical to each container of hot water.
3. Stir until chemicals are dissolved.
4. Add pinecones and soak overnight.
5. Allow pinecones to dry thoroughly in warm dry air for 2 days.

How to Use It:

Add cones to fire two or three at a time. The colorful flames will last only a short time.

Crystal Garden Solution

You Will Need:

several pieces of coal, charcoal briquettes, or some stones
shallow bowl
6 tablespoons salt
6 tablespoons bluing
6 tablespoons water
1 tablespoon ammonia
food coloring

Warning: Ammonia fumes can make some people ill. Keep the ammonia tightly capped and out of reach of small children.

How to Make It:

1. Place the coal or stones in the bottom of the shallow bowl.
2. Combine salt, bluing, water, and ammonia in a small bowl and mix well.
3. Pour mixture over coal or rocks.
4. Drop a few spots of different food coloring over the mixture.
5. Let stand a few hours. Crystals will begin to form. They will grow to be colorful and interesting for several days.

Newspaper Clipping Preservative

You Will Need:

1 quart warm club soda
    large bowl
1 milk of magnesia tablet
    large cookie sheet with sides
    newspaper clippings

How to Make It:

1. Pour the club soda into the bowl.
2. Drop the milk of magnesia tablet into the club soda and let sit overnight to dissolve.
3. Place the cookie sheet on a flat surface. Then pour in ¼ inch of preservative solution.
4. Place newspaper clippings in liquid and let set until thoroughly saturated.
5. Remove clippings and lay them out to dry on a flat surface.

Makes 1 quart.

How to Use It:

This preservative will prevent any clipping from turning yellow as long as the clipping is kept out of direct sunlight.

Recycled Paper

You Will Need:

> container large enough to hold paper to be used
> wastepaper such as tablet paper, newspaper, or computer
>   paper
> water
> ¼ cup bleach
> wire or plastic screen or nylon net
> light wooden frame (a splatter lid may be used for small
>   pieces)
> food processor or blender
> terry cloth towel
> sponge
> 2 pieces of board or Formica
> a heavy weight

Warning: Keep bleach out of the reach of children.

How to Make It:

1. Fill the container with water. (For whiter paper add ¼ cup bleach to soaking water.) Tear paper into tiny pieces and put into the container. Soak overnight.

2. In the meantime, tack the screen or nylon net to the wooden frame.

3. The next day, pour a little water into the food processor or blender. Set blender at liquify or use short pulses on food processor. Drop in the soaked paper, a little at a time, to keep the pulp from getting so thick it ruins the processor.

4. Pour the pulp onto the screen. Distribute evenly and smoothly over screen. Let drain.

5. After excess water drains out, gently roll pulp onto the

towel. Press with a sponge to remove as much water as possible.

6. Put the pulp between two pieces of board or Formica and place under something heavy to press. Leave to dry for several days.

How to Use It:

Recycled Paper is good for making paper sculptures or greeting cards.

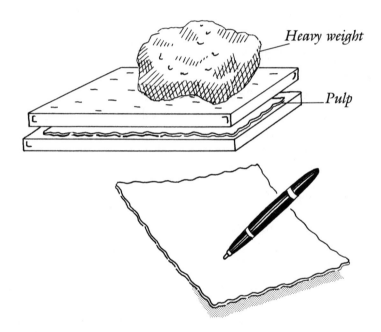

Heavy weight

Pulp

Index